Pencil Lady

Adventures of a High School Math Tutor

Emily Bunker

Artwork by John Bunker

emilybunker@alumni.stanford.edu

Cover design by R.E. Brodeur Printing

All photographs courtesy of the Bunker family archive

Independently published
Available from online bookstores

Here's to my students, for keeping me young
Each of you, truly, a hero unsung

Asking great questions; competing with flair
Solving equations; completing the square

Rapping, cartooning, and curves exponential
Hockey, quadratics, and hair quintessential

Pencils and paper and tests consequential
Happiness reigned when you reached your potential

And here's to you, Bob, for support never-ending
Such kindness and talent and friendship transcending

Emily Bunker

Cheers to all the teachers who give out pencils every single day, knowing that they'll never get them back.

Anonymous

Author's Note

In all chapters except for "The Sonoma Project," names were changed and some details – such as where and when the stories took place – were left out.

CONTENTS

INTRODUCTION

For fifteen years I was Pencil Lady, a dedicated high school tutor who always had a pencil (sharpened, of course!) to lend to a student. My focus was math and the SAT, but I spent many of those years as a general academic tutor too. Parents and the school district hired me for private and small group tutoring; I also worked as a math and physics teaching assistant at the high school for a year.

When I was in high school myself, I had a life-changing volunteer job that indirectly led to my tutoring work. I tell that story in the middle of the book.

After I'd begun tutoring English, Spanish, and history, I discovered I was good at math. The head guidance counselor mentioned there was a request for a math tutor (a common request, it turned out), and asked me if I wanted to give it a shot. I did – and loved it. I then got out the books and studied what I needed to know in order to switch gears.

These are the funny, surprising, heartbreaking, and inspiring things that happened in the midst of showing my students how to solve the puzzle of high school math. Or in the midst of giving them a pencil.

One

James and the Hockey Boys

In the beginning, James' hair alternated between spikey and flat. This changed his appearance so much that I didn't realize it was the same boy. Later on in the schoolyear, when his hair got too long for the gravity-defying look, he went platinum blonde. On the other side of the classroom was Ben, my former dental hygienist's nephew, with his standard-issue crewcut. James was a diminutive theater guy. Ben was a star athlete who played every sport.

These two ninth graders were as different as night and day, but they were both outgoing and very polite (although Ben's politeness was a bit much: think Eddie Haskell on *Leave It to Beaver*). And they were both good at math (although James only did well if you could get him to sit down long enough to actually do the math). I knew them because I was a teaching assistant in Mrs. Kelly's Algebra 1 class.

Ginger Hair Everywhere

That winter, the boys ice hockey team qualified for the state tournament. The players secretly decided to bleach their hair before the big event. A dash of ginger dye was added to the mix, creating a color you might describe as platinum with a twist of metallic tangerine. Looking at it was like looking at the sun: after a while, you had to look away. The plan was to take off the helmets in unison to reveal the hair at the end of the opening game . . . if they won. The crowd would go wild.

By the time I got to class the morning after the mass bleaching, I'd seen boys with ginger hair everywhere, and had been told the story. (The dazzling color was suddenly shorthand for "yep, I'm a hockey player.") I glanced across the room at James' no-longer-eye-catching hair and thought, *uh oh – I bet he doesn't like this.* Right on cue, he was complaining: "Everyone thinks I'm on the hockey team . . ." Ben said, "James: NO ONE thinks you're on the hockey team."

The following day, James had changed his tune. Rather than complain, he cheerfully announced, "I'm the captain of the hockey team!" Brief pause, then, "Not really! Just kidding!"

π

They lost the playoff game (5-2). So the helmets stayed put. But the boys had fun anyway, and they all agreed that the chance to wow the fans made the stunt worthwhile. Plus, they did get to show off their hair at the pre-game ceremony. Ben showed me a picture of them lined up, ready to play, with helmets in hand and hair aglow.

The Final Days of Ginger Hair

The ice hockey team's hair dye extravaganza was more or less history within a couple of weeks. One boy dyed his hair back to its original color. Another shaved it off. Ben, on the other hand, evidently liked the look: he let the ginger stay until his usual short haircuts did away with it.

As for James, he got tired of bleaching his hair. A horizontal line between the old (dark brown) and the new (ginger-free platinum) gradually grew out as summertime approached.

Two

Natalie's House

A ninth-grade girl was home recovering from mono. My job was to help with her schoolwork. I was the link between her and school: I turned in the work, talked to the teachers, and taught lessons as needed. I could wing most subjects, but if a student needed help that I couldn't provide, a second tutor would be hired; this time, someone else handled science.

Natalie and I worked at the kitchen table, with Sherlock, her enormous hermit crab, between us in his "condo" (a cute little terrarium). Their lovable dog, and a flock of chickens roaming free in the backyard, completed the menagerie. Off and on, her mother (a visiting nurse) and father (a school bus driver) were there. I was soon to learn that the kitchen was the center of family life, which carried on despite a tutorial supposedly taking place. The drama! The comedy! And I don't mean the chance disagreement or humorous remark. I'm talking about rip-roaring arguments — *they know I'm here, right?* — and laugh-out-loud hilarity.

From the jaw-dropping: Mom telling the tale of walking for hours through deep snow to visit patients, since the roads were impassable . . . to the eye-opening: Dad explaining the controversy over seatbelts on school buses . . . and from the mundane: Natalie being yelled at for polishing off the cookies . . . to the macabre: me listening to the gory details of the previous night (foxes killed the chickens).

Whatever the topic of conversation, love and respect were in the air. It was the place to be – the real deal.

One afternoon, Natalie suddenly said, "Do you hear that?" Wafting in from the back of the house was the theme song from M*A*S*H. She explained that her dad wasn't happy about paying for this new thing called streaming – until he learned he could now watch his favorite TV show whenever he felt like it. After the episode, he wandered into the kitchen to grab a bite to eat. "I hear you're watching M*A*S*H again," his daughter gently teased. "Well, it's a good show!" he replied in a charming huff.

Her artistic talent got my attention immediately. For an English assignment, she made a spectacularly original storyboard about the Hitchcock thriller *Rear Window*. I recommended it from her teacher's list of suggestions; she watched the movie and was sold.

Purple Hair

Once Natalie started feeling better, her natural exuberance returned, and she dyed her hair purple. She was going to be reciting a Shakespeare monologue when she got back, so she practiced and practiced with her renewed enthusiasm. She'd get close to the finish line, forget a word, and then cheerfully go all the way back to the beginning.

On the last day, they gave me a carton of pre-fox-attack eggs, and I gave Natalie a poem I'd written for her (see page 8).

What an experience, this fiesta of fun and philosophy. They cracked me up and they inspired me. I saw Natalie at school, with blue hair now, a few days later. Shouting "Emilyyyy!!" for all the world to hear, she ran over and gave me a big hug.

Unfortunate Math Test

Everyone at school missed her. At the halfway point of her absence, her ancient old-school English teacher told her that things were *so boring* without her: dependable proof that the girl could simultaneously rock the boat and win people over.

She was scheduled to return to her math class on a test day. I knew that, so I asked her guidance counselor if she should wait until the following day since she wasn't quite caught up to the rest of the class. "Don't worry," he said, "because under these circumstances, teachers let students ease back in." The teacher seemed to have missed that memo because he gave her the test. Which she failed. And which left her in a puddle of tears. I found out from her mom.

This sad turn of events caused a huge brouhaha between the teacher and me. A year and a half later, I got the teaching assistant job and was assigned to one of his classes. *Oh no!* Mr. Callaghan and I had communicated via email only, so he didn't know what I looked like. *Perhaps, fingers crossed, he forgot my name.* I never could tell if he made the connection; he didn't ever mention the run-in, and no way was I going to. I dreaded having to work in his classroom, and expected the worst, but I was mistaken. I came to have a tremendous amount of respect for Mr. Callaghan (chapter 14).

She got to retake that test. I like to think it was at least partly due to my intervention, but that's another thing I'll never know.

π

During my teaching assistant year, in the stairwell of the library building, a voice behind me quietly, almost shyly, said, "Hi Emily." The voice belonged to someone whose hair was a color you could be born with, so I almost didn't recognize my dear old student. It was great to catch up. Two years had gone by since her bout with mono took her out of school.

Looking back, I marvel at Natalie's sunny disposition. I'm reminded of my sister's friend who was known for living joyfully. When asked how he did it, he would say, "I tried it the other way, and I didn't like it."

In a one-of-a-kind family scene
I tutored a girl who had mono
Alongside our daily routine
Sherlock was snug in his condo

Her hair was a sort of light brown
But when she got better, she dyed it
A bow when she went on the town
To her bright purple hair, she tied it

She's an artist extraordinaire
Right away, I got that impression
Rear Window uncovered her flair
For creative artistic expression

Reciting the long Shakespeare speech
For suspense, this was second to none
The ending would be within reach
Then oh dear! it was back to line one

From English to Spanish to math
We scrambled to get it all done
I guided her down the best path
While having a whole lot of fun

Three

Extraterrestrial Cartooning

William was in one of my two slower-paced math classes. He kept to himself, and kept his fedora and long black overcoat on. Always. (I don't remember him without these accessories, but I imagine they were absent when it was warm out.) At his desk near the door, his imposing frame partially hidden under his hat and coat, he'd dive back into his drawings of extraterrestrials the minute his schoolwork was done.

When an assignment involved individual whiteboards, Mrs. Simms gave him a second one for his artwork. So instead of an E.T. or two (or six or seven) in pencil in the margin of his notebook, the sensational creatures materialized on his extra whiteboard in red, blue, green, or purple, depending on the marker he was given.

These were no ordinary extraterrestrials! They were brilliant. The work of an artist. It so happened that I needed an illustrator for a book I was writing; I was thinking of offering the job to William. First, I checked if we were allowed to hire students. The vice principal, who hardly batted an eye at my question (William was famous), told me it was fine. He said that students were hired all the time, especially for their art.

Next, I asked the artist himself. His shyness didn't stop him from smiling at my offer (I had never seen him smile!). We discussed the details, and I showed him pictures to give him an idea of what I needed. No aliens from outer space – most of them were plants – but I figured he could do anything.

In the end, he decided to turn the job down. "I'm a cartoonist," he said, by way of explanation. This was *not* said with an apologetic "that's all I can do" tone of voice. Rather, his answer had an unmistakable air of self-confidence about it. He was proud of what he did.

I was sorry it didn't work out, but also impressed that someone so young knew who he was and what he was good at.

Four

The Mavericks

The school district hired me to tutor a girl with a long-term suspension. Her future at the high school was in limbo, but in the meantime, she needed help with her homework.

Parking on a windswept patch of rocks and dirt, and walking to the front door of Rose's mobile home . . . those moments are seared in my memory because it was my very first day as a tutor. There's a snapshot in my mind – who knows if it's accurate – of a table already set for dinner, with olive green napkins placed neatly inside napkin rings on flowery placemats. We worked at the dinner table that first day, and then switched to meeting at the town library. I brought her a gift: a fancy bar of rose soap, which, as I'd hoped, got things off to a great start.

In a matter of weeks, Rose's pal Anna was suspended. Two girls were now teetering on the edge. I wasn't told the story behind either suspension, but whatever happened, it seemed to me the bigger picture was that they were too independent for formal schooling. Neither one of them presented herself as unconventional: no eccentric hair, offbeat clothes, piercings, or tattoos. They were mavericks on the inside only.

Finding Her Way

Anna, who was born the same day as my daughter Michelle, was my student for a long time. For months I was a fixture at her house. We started with schoolwork – but then she suddenly dropped out of school. She wanted to get her GED (high school equivalency diploma) instead, so I overhauled our course of action. The school district agreed to keep paying me temporarily; when the money ran out, it became a volunteer job.

I learned about the exam. Together we explored the subjects. She did worksheet after worksheet, practice test after practice test. (I'll never forget her pencils: they were spotted with cat teeth marks, and may or may not have ever come in contact with a regulation pencil sharpener.) I drove her to the official practice tests, which went off without a hitch.

We were home free. Or so I thought.

Anna's focus began to drift away. A couple of times I arrived to an empty house. Wondering if we were wasting our time, I had a talk with her and her mom; normally I'm very low-key, but I managed to find the wherewithal to (calmly) lay it on the line. With eyes on the floor, they didn't say a word. It was smooth sailing after that.

Finally, the time came to put it to the test . . .

This was a multi-day event. Each day, after dropping her off, I sat in the waiting room (her mom's work schedule kept her from doing any of the driving). I wasn't too worried because she was well prepared and, if I remember correctly, cool as a cucumber. Test-taking anxiety was not an issue for her. Sure enough: success! I was so proud of her. Of us both.

I ran into the freshly minted graduate a short time later, and she looked very happy. I got updates, all positive, for years because her mom worked at a store I shopped at regularly.

Recently, Rose and I crossed paths for the first time since I was her tutor. My daughter Eliza and I were having dinner at our local Mexican restaurant, and she brought us our tacos and margaritas. I was thrilled to find out that she was doing well and brimming with exciting plans for herself.

π

After hearing some of my stories, my brother liked to joke that the girls at the high school might start causing trouble on purpose so they could finish their education with me.

Five

Pencil Time

More and more schoolwork was being done on iPads, which were loaned out to the students for the year (this major shift was new – the program was only in its third year). Pencils, however, were still required for math class. Not that the requirement wasn't frequently ignored.

Pencil Lady to the rescue.

A classroom assistant with plenty of nicely sharpened pencils in her briefcase probably ruined any chance that the errant students would ever get into the pencil-packing habit themselves. Hmm. But that detail wasn't about to stop me. I liked offering this self-assigned service, and sometimes I even got the pencil back. When I'm at home working on a project for which a pencil works best, a long row of sharp No. 2 Dixon Ticonderogas of various lengths – erasers worn down on the short ones – awaits me. As one gets dull, it's on to the next.

Borrowing Pencils

A tall skinny guy who sat in front of me in Mr. Hart's Algebra 1 class only *thought* he wasn't good at math. Nate actually had a lot of natural talent for the subject – he just needed assistance. He also needed a pencil. Soon enough, all he had to do was turn around and look at me sheepishly. No words necessary. And there was a silver lining: his grades were improving because math tips went along with the pencils.

Meanwhile, time flew by thanks to Mr. Hart's kooky sense of humor. "The dark side," for example, was negative numbers. He liked to regale us with stories about the bleak futures he imagined for his students who didn't keep their noses to the grindstone. One story had studious Holly and Josh married and out for a Sunday drive (torrents of laughter: rumor had it they liked each other) ten years hence. As they're moseying along, they see Al and Dan (included in the vignette because they'd been coming to class late and/or weren't doing their homework) up ahead *minding their lemonade stand*. Holly says, "Hey Josh, let's buy some lemonade and help them out!"

π

I surprised Nate the last day of school. Right before the usual pencil-borrowing time, I walked around to the front of his desk and handed him two brand-new, nicely sharpened No. 2 Ticonderoga pencils. "These are for you," I said.

He looked up. Again, no words necessary: appreciation was already written on his face. (In pencil.)

Six

Two Girls at the Corner

The Friendly One

I helped ninth graders with their math and physics homework in a study skills class. The questions I got from a hardworking girl named Ivy were surprisingly sophisticated. She was already an A student; her goal was to keep from plummeting down to the A– range.

Aware that her level of questioning should take a backseat to the more pressing concerns of her fellow classmates, Ivy first made absolutely certain I wasn't busy. Once she was sure I was free – it was tricky to convince her she wasn't bothering me – we'd launch into discussions of the finer points of, say, factoring differences of squares or solving linear inequalities.

One day, I asked her why she was in study skills. She didn't seem to belong there. She explained that math and science came to her naturally, but not language arts or social studies. She didn't like those subjects very much because you have to memorize facts and points of view that are constantly changing. "Math is different," she said wistfully, "because two plus two is always four."

The Aloof One

Ivy's friend Jill struggled mightily with algebra, and detested it, but she wanted to be left alone. She would glare at me if I made a suggestion, assuring my hasty retreat; she insisted on doing her homework by herself even when she didn't have the foggiest idea how to do it. This was alarming because she was on the verge of failing.

The three of us sat together at the corner of a large table. It was odd: while one waited patiently for me, in hopes of staying on top of her game, the other actively avoided me – perhaps thinking that math might go away if I was ignored long enough.

I wouldn't have minded ignoring Jill back (my feelings were ruffled), but I knew I should keep trying to reach her. *Wait a minute . . . I have an idea.* She loved horses, and I had a horse from seventh to eleventh grade. I brought in a picture of 12-year-old me riding my beloved Hula, and what do you know? The ice was broken.

Next: refine *how* to help, now that I was allowed in the door. Tiny slivers of advice casually tossed her way seemed to work pretty well (as long as I limited it to once or twice per class). Bit by bit, she let me show her things. Not that she wanted to! Jill was visibly resisting her natural tendencies. Impressive that she was making a valiant effort to change her ways.

The picture I showed Jill – Hula and me in 1967 at what was then called Stanford Riding Stables

Seven

The Apology

Two or three months into the schoolyear, Carlos transferred to our high school – from the Philippines, I think. He was placed in the more advanced of my two slower-paced classes. He seemed lost, so together we reviewed the basics; it didn't take him long to catch up to the rest of the class, but he remained slightly off balance.

Then suddenly, without warning, cautiousness turned into confidence. Math was clicking for him now, and he enjoyed speaking up whenever he knew the answer. Mrs. Simms expected students to raise their hands. No blurting. "Don't be a blurter!" she would say. Carlos was in trouble almost daily because his enthusiasm tended to get the better of him.

Next, also out of the blue, he got smart-alecky. He texted his friends: against classroom rules. He sneaked in ice cream, meaning he'd left school (in order to buy it): against school rules. I tried reasoning with him, but he just laughed it off. He was having a marvelous time tempting fate.

Several of the others, particularly Hazel, a sweet girl who was psyched about math, occupied my time as well. I forget what caused Carlos to snap at me, but it might have been because I was busy with Hazel and he was getting impatient. His nasty remark was stunning because I always treated him with the utmost respect.

A day or so later, he looked for me at lunchtime. With more maturity than most adults have, he told me, at length, how sorry he was. I assured him it was okay.

Fun Corner

Everything returned to normal again in the extra-help corner of the room (the "fun corner," as Carlos called it, where you could borrow the teaching assistant's ultra-cool calculator). He cut out the wisenheimer stuff. The newest member of class had taken a look at his own behavior, didn't like what he saw, and chose to do something about it.

Without demanding, or even asking for, an apology, I was offered one. So it was genuine . . . and therefore meaningful.

The Sonoma Project

In March 1972, when I was 16 and a junior in high school, my friend Martha told me about a volunteer program called The Sonoma Project. High school students from Palo Alto, California, were spending weekends and vacations at Sonoma State Hospital – in a dormitory that was originally a cow barn – planning and carrying out activities for the residents. I was intrigued. That weekend, in a large institution-green stick-shift van that had THE SONOMA PROJECT painted on the outside, I was on my way to beautiful Sonoma Valley.

Once Upon a Time in Oak Lodge

When we arrived, well into the evening, we headed straight for Oak Lodge – a popular residence where volunteers were welcome at any time. In a flash, we were surrounded by boys positively over the moon to have a break from the usual routine. I was nervous, but Martha reassured me.

In the morning I took Freddy, a high-octane little guy from Oak Lodge, out for some fresh air. As we walked and ran and skipped, I asked if he wanted to make up a story. I said I'd write it down. He liked that idea, so we skedaddled over to the Volunteer Village (cow barn dorm) to get something to write with (I wasn't Pencil Lady yet).

Thrilled to have the attention of all the volunteers, Freddy began: "Once upon a time, there was a little girl." I wrote this down. He stopped and thought for a moment. "Once upon a time, there was a little boy." I wrote again; he paused again. "Once upon a time, there was a BIG MONSTER!"

He took the pen from me and wrote "once upon a time" . . .

Then wrote his name and, with help, my name . . .

FRED

EMILY

And he drew pictures . . .

Then the record player caught his eye. I put on "Oldies but Goodies," and he sang along with pizzazz, using his fist as a microphone. When our impromptu party came to an end, Freddy and I skipped back to Oak Lodge belting out "I've Been Working on the Railroad" again and again at the top of our lungs.

The Volunteer Village – our converted cow barn

Angels

One of our jobs was feeding people with severe disabilities. Unable to do anything for themselves, they spent their lives lying helplessly in bed. We would show up at dinnertime, and the employees would review the proper techniques, assign someone to each of us, and pass out the puréed food.

A Bach record that began with "Jesu, Joy of Man's Desiring" was always playing in the background. This exquisite music had a calming effect on the residents. I only know what it was because, having grown to love it, I checked the label one day and then bought myself a copy. Now whenever I play the record, I think of the angelic caretakers who offered soothing music and a gentle touch, every day without fail, to those who didn't have much else to live for.

Bane Cottage

Ping Pong and Bones

Playing ping pong at Bane Cottage was one of our favorite activities. We could tell ourselves we were doing a good deed when in fact we were simply having some fun. Various combinations of residents, staff, and volunteers would likely be, on any given day, in hot pursuit of a ping pong victory.

Tom, a regular at the ping pong table, was very capable: he easily could have been living and working "on the outside." He had a magnetic personality – funny and full of joy – and was musically gifted . . .

Tom was a topnotch "bones" player. The bones are a folk percussion instrument traditionally made from animal shins or ribs cut to the right length, cleaned, and bleached in the sun. The player holds two curved pieces between the fingers, with convex sides together. The bones are the second oldest musical instrument, after the human voice, and are played worldwide in a huge variety of music. European immigrants are believed to have brought them to the New World. They are "idiophones"; that is, the sound comes from the material they're made out of, which today includes wood and plastic.

I'd never even heard of the bones when I first saw Tom and some of the other residents, many of whom had Down syndrome, playing along with the radio. They were keeping the beat with an easy-breezy clackety-clack. George, a longhaired, tie-dyed psych tech (psychiatric technician) who worked the swing shift, explained to me that the flexibility of the hands of people with Down syndrome makes them natural candidates for learning to play the bones.

The bones players of Bane – Tom is second from right

Years later, I ran into George. He told me Tom had died but not before getting a chance to live and work on the outside.

Sonoma State Hospital, called Sonoma Developmental Center since 1986, closed down on December 31, 2018 (while I was writing this!). From 2015 to the very end, the residents were gradually transitioned to new homes. What to do next with the place – more than a hundred buildings, all in need of repair, on eight hundred and sixty acres of land bordering Jack London State Historic Park – was still undecided when the institution closed.

I was a Sonoma Project volunteer for a year and a half. I was the chairperson towards the end; one of my responsibilities, if our houseparent wasn't available to do it, was driving the volunteers up and back in that large institution-green stick-shift van. I really enjoyed this. The van had a "3-on-the-tree" transmission (three gears; stick on the steering column).

Horses grazing near the Volunteer Village

I sometimes wonder if we made much of a difference. But even though the contributions of our motley crew of volunteers were probably a drop in the bucket, I'll always have my memories . . . of spunky storytelling, angelic caretaking, and those phenomenal bones players of Bane.

The experience inspired me to learn how to teach. I've had teaching jobs off and on my entire life: besides the tutoring, I've worked as an assistant for disabled children, and taught and choreographed high school dance classes and musicals.

Tom and me in 1973
at what was then called Sonoma State Hospital

Eight

Physics with Leyla

She was a 4-year-old orphan in Central Asia when she was adopted by an American family and brought to the United States. The traumas she endured before being adopted damaged her memory. Test-taking was therefore a tremendous challenge. Her bubbly personality and air of sophistication, however, disguised the blurry confusion and scrambled facts that were lurking beneath the surface.

Setting the Stage

I didn't know a proton from an electron. And yet, I was assigned to a physics student who needed extra help. *Oh dear*. Next thing I knew, it was day one of Introductory Physics, and I was being introduced to physics and to a tall, striking beauty named Leyla.

Mr. Romo was funny and smart and full of wild enthusiasm. His class was a revelation. It wasn't just his teaching – it was also how he interacted with the kids: with kindness, understanding, and an effective no-nonsense toughness as needed. Here was a teacher who loved to teach. I felt lucky to be one of his students (granted, one who must stay a step ahead, in order to pretend to know stuff). The hip, sometimes edgy, music softly playing in the background set the stage perfectly for the interesting ideas and discoveries in the foreground.

Borrowing Erasers

Leyla and I got along wonderfully. We enjoyed comparing, and occasionally debating, our answers. She had pencils but no erasers, so that's what *she* would borrow; a decent eraser was essential because the appearance of the finished product was important to her. She was in my study skills class, so we could continue on there when necessary.

It was actually better that I didn't have all the answers – I'd track down whatever I didn't know – because less difference between us translated to more confidence for her. Not only that, but the tables were turned when it came to the computer technology we used for experiments. Computers aren't my strong point, so she was ahead of me on that count.

Because of her testing issues, I was permitted some leeway. We'd retreat to a separate room, where I could clarify questions and even give a few small hints. This flexible approach was encouraged, unlike a similarly unique situation with another student (chapter 15). The result was test grades that corresponded reasonably well to Leyla's talents and strong work ethic. The alternative, rigidity, would not have helped her one iota.

Our Favorite Class

Leyla thanked me sweetly after the final. Later I thought, *oh darn! I wish I'd let her know it was my favorite class.* Why my favorite? Because of the magnificent combination of subject (fascinating), teacher (amazing), and student (delightful).

I got my chance the next day when I passed her in the hallway between classes. Her face lit up, and she told me it was her favorite class too.

Nine

A Quiet Island

Amid the zany shenanigans of Ben and James' class (chapter 1) was a quiet island of one: a Cary Grant lookalike named Sam. He sat right in the middle of the room. The class was ninety percent boys, ninety percent of whom were loud and untamable; Ivy and Jill (chapter 6) were two of three girls. During independent study – which was when it got especially noisy in there, with heated debates on topics like who, if anyone, thinks James is on the hockey team – Sam would listen to music (with earphones) while solemnly studying.

He could have used help, but attention seemed to embarrass him. He didn't smile. He didn't look up. Not even when we were doing really fun stuff like practicing the quadratic formula to the tune of "Pop! Goes the Weasel" . . .

$$\frac{-b \pm \sqrt{b^2 - 4ac}}{2a}$$

Ne-ga-tive b plus or mi-NUS
The square root of b squared
Minus four a-a-a c
ALL over two a

That wasn't the only nifty memorization trick Mrs. Kelly had up her sleeve. Another one helped her students remember which line, vertical or horizontal, has a slope of zero. People tend to mix this up – picking the correct one can be a crapshoot. Whenever she was talking about slope, therefore, she wrote "horizontal" like this:

*hori*Z*ontal*

π

Throughout it all, Sam remained quiet. Until he didn't.

It was close to summer vacation. I think the dramatic shift occurred when he managed to solve an unusually complicated math problem on his own. Like dominoes, success begat further success. Which led to a deluge (no exaggeration) of friendly conversation. Then he decided to move to the back of the classroom, where I sat, so he could more easily check if his answers were right or wrong.

In the words of lyricist Howard Ashman in the musical *Little Shop of Horrors*, "Don't it go to show ya never know."

Ten

Anatomy of a Train Wreck

Because I'm a misfit myself, the kids I connected with best were the misfits. Any type would do. *New student isn't in the in-crowd? Great!* And we'd be off and running. Still, I usually got along perfectly well with the non-misfit set.

Another inconsistency in my tutoring was not always being specific or firm enough about what I expected the student to do ahead of time (this didn't apply to my classroom work). A lot can still be accomplished if a student isn't prepared, but in some cases, expectations and consequences – for example, cancelling the appointment if she/he shows up without having done the assignment – are necessary.

Kate, a pretty in-crowd girl, was the unlucky recipient of the intersection of these two shortcomings of mine. Her parents had hired me to help her navigate Algebra 2.

She would arrive having understood almost nothing in math class all week, so I would scramble to explain the entire week in one hour. It was a race against time, and the clock wasn't sympathetic. If, on the other hand, I'd given her homework (such as: "take a look at last week's lessons, and pick three or four topics that are hard for you"), she might have been able to nail down a few things. As it was, the information wasn't sticking because there was no time left for reinforcing it.

Even without assigning homework, I could've at least selected a few items myself and focused there. That's less effective (if students mull a concept over *before* a lesson, some ground has already been covered – so they understand it faster), but those items would have fared better singled out than awhirl in a sea of other math minutiae.

Either way – require her to prepare or pick the topics myself – we certainly wouldn't have been able to get to everything, and I would've recognized early on that one tutorial a week was not going to make a dent. I would have explained this to Kate's parents. They, in turn, might have investigated a lower-level class, the free afterschool help that teachers and students offered, or both. (More than one day per week with a private tutor was generally considered to be too expensive.)

Of course, they could have gone that route anyway, and for all I know, perhaps they did look into the alternatives. I do know that Kate tried and failed to transfer to a comparable class taught by someone else – she vehemently disliked her teacher – but there wasn't one that fit into her schedule.

Her grades were improving in the beginning, so we were all lulled into a false sense of security. Then it quietly started to slip away. It was a slow-motion train wreck. She didn't fail, but her final grade was disappointing, and she and her parents were understandably upset with me.

π

Rushing through the whole shebang each week at breakneck speed guaranteed that little would sink in. My feeble excuse is that I had never encountered such a scenario, but I should have stopped for half a minute to find another way. Instead, I stubbornly and uncreatively thought there wasn't one.

Maybe if I just keep at it, this useless approach will (all by itself!) become a winning approach.

The misfit/in-crowd thing compounded the sorry situation. I was painfully aware that we never really hit it off.

Kate's guidance counselor (the head of the department – the person who, years earlier, asked if I wanted to try tutoring math) didn't blame me. In fact, she took it with a grain of salt. I guess in a job like hers, dramas large and small go with the territory. Her belief in me never wavered, and for that I was, and still am, grateful.

Eleven

Four Kinds of Pain

The Twins

One of my first students who needed to be tutored at home for a medical reason was in psychological pain, not physical pain. He was constantly being bullied, and had reached the breaking point. I taught him algebra for the majority of one schoolyear. They lived in my hometown.

Around that time, there was another terribly sad story . . .

Jake was suffering from a hereditary degenerative disease. It had gotten to the point where he couldn't attend school, so I was hired to tutor him at his house three times a week. We divvied up the time and covered all the classes – and had a great time in the process. I remember a gigantic project that I hand-delivered, I think to his science teacher.

His twin brother, Ezra, seemed to have escaped Jake's fate. They hardly looked like twins: one was small and extremely thin; the other, big and robust. I was warmly welcomed into their home and treated like a member of the family, just as I was at Natalie's house many years later (chapter 2).

Jake's health eventually stabilized enough for him to return to school part-time. Once in a while we ran into each other there, as well as in the coffee shop where he worked. It was always nice to have a chance to chat.

Tragically, Ezra ended up with the disease too. Last I heard, it wasn't severe enough to keep him out of school.

The Animal Lover

I learned about the goth look when the school district hired me to tutor Carly. Her black clothes, hair, and makeup were highlighted with splashes of color (pink, typically) here and there. The effect was mesmerizing: you couldn't resist sneaking a second look. Underneath all that was a girl who loved animals. In fact, a love of animals is what led her to me.

Carly had swerved to avoid hitting an opossum in the road, totaling her car and practically totaling herself. Her head was badly injured, and her memory was damaged. When she was healthy enough to give schoolwork a try, after many months of rehab, we were assigned to work together. We got along swimmingly from the start. She became a family friend, not just my student. In time, she recovered her ability to think clearly and to remember things.

And then she swerved to miss another animal. She crashed the car, but thank goodness, she was okay.

The Landscaper

Rick wanted to leave his hometown after high school graduation. The answer, he decided, was to join the Marines. One problem: he was having trouble with the entrance exam.

That was when I came aboard. I helped him prepare for the online test six ways from Sunday – but it was no use. After several attempts, we were forced to admit defeat. I thought, *there might be a silver lining here because "in order to go away" doesn't seem like a great reason to join the Marines.*

And naturally, I wondered if the setback had saved his life.

Years went by. Then one day, I got a surprising phone call. Rick had started a landscaping business, and wanted to hire me to teach him how to calculate the areas of front and back yards. *Those* tutorials were a big success. Hallelujah!

While learning how to figure out the size of his customers' outdoor spaces, he mentioned that he was glad he didn't get into the Marines.

Twelve

Crazy Cat Ladies

Charlotte was another student of mine with a medical leave of absence. She was getting devastating headaches caused by multiple concussions. The most recent: a rock in someone's backpack on the bus whacked her in the head. Truly bizarre.

She and I worked together for an entire year – October to September – on Spanish, English, and a lot of Algebra 2. As usual for medical absences, I was hired by the school district. We were a team whose goal was to FINISH JUNIOR YEAR. She did attend the occasional class, but very rarely, because noise and crowds made her headaches worse. Digital screens were off limits too (staring at them caused her head to split), and as it happened, smart boards were the name of the game in the classroom now.*

---

* Smart boards – interactive whiteboards that do more than you can possibly imagine – have to be seen to be believed. Suffice it to say, substitute teachers kept their distance. I hadn't seen them yet when I was working with Charlotte, so I only knew there was some mystical screen she had to avoid. The classroom assistant job was later; then I saw the magic for myself. In that position I didn't need to know how to use them, but every so often I had to deal with one anyway . . . the students thoroughly enjoyed telling me what to do.

Even in the peace and quiet of her own home, she frequently couldn't concentrate. Some days, the relentless headaches were mild enough for us to finish the work, with or without an ice-cold water bottle pressed to her forehead. Other days, we'd have to quit early. Once, I arrived to find her feeling so miserable that we couldn't do any work at all.

Her sister's unsuccessful attempts to pass the driver's license exam punctuated the headache saga. Charlotte got a "failed again" text message one day. We felt bad for her, of course, but any diversion was welcome. (She did finally pass.)

Another interesting diversion occurred when their deck was in danger of collapsing due to the unusual amount of snow that had accumulated. A couple of big strong neighborhood men lead the way; Charlotte, her mom, and I did our best to keep up. We shoveled a lot of snow! It was fun though, and we were able to rescue the deck.

Being Oranged

Things we had in common: we both preferred to wear jeans and T-shirts, and we were both cat crazy . . .

One of hers, a rather sociable fellow, liked to sprawl across my open math book. I'd have to peek under him and over him to see what I was doing. If I wasn't careful, my parabola might have turned into a hyperbola. By the end of the hour

I was bedecked with orange fur; as my friend Sherry would say, I was "oranged." (She has an orange tabby too.)

I was always on the lookout for opportunities to cheer her up. I have a refrigerator magnet with a picture of a dog and a cat sitting at desks in a classroom. They're hard at work solving the math problem on the blackboard (2 + 3 =), looking tired and stressed out. The caption: **against animal testing**. I brought it in – she laughed a lot.

Her passion for animals inspired her to tackle (for her first English project) the question of whether or not zoos could still be justified. I googled the topic and found mountains of information, which I read aloud. Fascinating conversations were followed by hours of dictation.* Our modus operandi was certainly painstaking, but that was our only option. Later in the year, she was able to handle digital screens for small stretches of time.

π

Charlotte finished everything, but just barely. She was given until the first day of the new schoolyear, and that's the day I turned in her last assignments.

---

* Thank you, seventh-grade typing teacher, wherever you may be! We were taught to use all our fingers, so I can zip right along. I always say (only half jokingly) that it's all I remember from school.

We were thrilled and relieved. We felt as though we'd run a marathon – one whose endpoint was not always in our line of vision. Then the time came to say goodbye.

I gave her a T-shirt with the words "Simple Math" at the top and a drawing of a graph underneath. The *x* axis is "Number of Cats," the *y* axis is "Crazy," and the line indicates what we all know: the more cats you have, the crazier you become.

She loved it. I got myself one too.

π

My mom died that August, at the age of 91. Charlotte didn't shy away. She told me how sorry she was, looking right into my eyes, and gave me a beautiful and inspirational card.

The soft-spoken girl with the freckly face was healthy enough to do senior year at school. She graduated with her class and went right to college. As far as I know, the friendly cat who oranged me once upon a time is still going strong.

Thirteen

Got Pi?

I taught SAT prep for years. In the beginning, as I dissected the test, I came to the realization that most of the questions were puzzles. Especially the math, but in one way or another this was true for every section. Also, the harder the question, the more puzzly it was. The stupid scary test was just a game! I was shocked. And so, being a devoted puzzler, teaching the SAT – the old versions, that is, before the dramatic overhaul in 2016 – made perfect sense.*

When I pointed out the tricks, traps, and shortcuts, students were stunned: "You've got to be kidding. You can *do* that?" Lightbulb moments happened all the time, and they were a sight to behold. Those who had the puzzle gene could jump right in, but people who were more comfortable methodically following the rules they had been taught – unless they had gobs of time to practice these new "secret" rules – generally didn't get as good a score as they should have. This was incredibly unfair, and a common criticism of the old SAT.

---

* I took it in high school, but since SAT prep wasn't a thing yet (this was the early seventies), I was bewildered and horrified, and subsequently blocked the experience out.

Hmmm, I wonder which way is best . . .

There were shortcuts galore on the old SAT.
The trick was to recognize them.

Michael was an A student in calculus. I didn't know what he was talking about half the time because I didn't get that far in math. His parents hired me.

He was the careful, deliberate kind of problem solver, so the fast and furious style that was the key to acing the old SAT didn't come naturally. With unlimited time, he'd have been able to solve just about anything by hook or by crook. ("Just about" means that some problems *simply could not* be solved by following the rules.) But in order not to run out of time, the shortcuts – most of which flew in the face of traditional math techniques – were essential ingredients.

Intrigued by my reckless and rule-free bag of tricks, Michael did his best to master them. "Hey, Bunker! Let me have another example of the triangular shortcut," he might say. Unfortunately, his busy schedule prevented him from practicing enough for the new approach to become second nature. His score did improve, but not as much as he had hoped.

His score should have been higher. Feeling frustrated, I ran the issue by my ex-husband, a math and science guy. He has an interesting theory. He believes these opposing math styles are innate, and that the slow-and-steady-wins-the-race people (he's one of them) are better suited to be scientists, while the fly-by-the-seat-of-your-pants types make better engineers.

Michael liked the theory, and it definitely softened the blow.

These three anecdotes are from *Secret Rules of the SAT Game: A Player's Guide*, a prep book I wrote for the old SAT:

. . . His test-taking anxiety bordered on brain freeze. I asked what he does when things go wrong onstage (he was an actor). He said, "I just deal with it." So I said, "Stage fright and test anxiety are essentially the same thing. If it feels like the sky is falling during the test, you can 'just deal' with that too. Rather than panic, take one tiny step at a time – and as matter-of-factly as possible. If you're totally stuck, pass the question and come back later if you have time. After temporarily putting a confusing question aside, you might see it in a new light and be able to tackle it after all." He was skeptical but willing to try. He reported afterwards that he'd managed his anxiety pretty well.

. . . She looked at me with an expression that said, *I challenge you to say something worthwhile.* She made me nervous! Then, out of nowhere, the quirkiness of SAT math started making sense to her. She changed her mind about my class.

. . . A mother called before the first day of SAT prep to tell me that her son was very smart but didn't want anyone to know it. He showed up looking coolly unimpressed. Week after week, he never said a word. But then, halfway through the course, he broke his silence and kindly explained a problem to a fellow classmate. He was relaxed and helpful from that moment on; I guess he decided it was okay to be smart.

This pep talk is from *Got Pi?*, another SAT book I wrote:

S·A·T \es-ā-'tē\

noun a puzzle masquerading as a college entrance exam
synonym see "3.75-hour college entrance exam that ironically isn't capable of predicting college success"

The SAT is more like a puzzle than any test you've ever taken. You're about to discover how to quickly, accurately, and elegantly solve the math variety. (Puzzles are supposed to be fun, and in fact a lot of this would be, if it wasn't the SAT.) Test-*takers* would benefit by understanding the minds of the test-*makers*. Are you willing to believe that they only pretend to care about Math Class Methods? Will do their best to lure you to an incorrect answer? Have created a thousand ways to waste your time? If so, prepare accordingly and you'll greatly increase your chances of getting the score you deserve.

Why Pi?

(a.k.a. π . . . a.k.a. 3.14159265358979323846264338 32 . . .)

Triangles are the SAT's favorite shape, but circles run a close second. Pi – the ratio of every circle's (yup, all of them) circumference to its diameter – is therefore a big deal on the test. International Pi Day is, of course, March 14 (if you're not sure why, check pi's digits above). Participants engage in pi-related activities and enjoy a piece of pie.

Have some pi pie on Pi Day (3/14)

Fourteen

Factoring: The Movie

Mr. Callaghan was always dreaming up interesting hands-on projects so that his students, alone or in small groups, could mess around with the lesson of the day. He recognized this as the approach that leads to actual learning. Sitting motionless while the teacher drones on doesn't come close; sooner or later the minds of even the most dedicated students float away to a distant time zone. After his students discovered the basic principles for themselves, he would give a presentation. His explanations were highly creative too. Maybe still boring for some, but at least the information had a reasonable chance of sticking around.

One project involved comparing arm span to height. Measuring tape was passed out, and they were off like a shot! Everyone got measured – it was pandemonium – and the results were graphed and analyzed. What made the exercise so good? Simple: the kids were invested in the outcome.

Mr. Callaghan had a tendency to be grumpy, however, and wasn't great at dealing with the natural rambunctiousness of ninth graders. He'd yell at them, and then, after a moment of stunned silence, they'd return to the important business of causing havoc. This was such a shame because his excellent teaching would get overshadowed. Sometimes I wanted to jump up and shout, "You don't know how lucky you are to have Mr. Callaghan as a teacher! Pay attention!"

π

The biggest and most entertaining project of the year – for the participants as well as those of us who had the honor of being in the audience – was called "Factoring: The Movie." In teams of three or four, they had to make a video of themselves teaching how to factor quadratic equations. Obviously everything had to be correct, but the grade would be better if it was clever and fun. One factoring movie after the next, ranging from fair to fairly awful (but still entertaining), was shown over the course of several days.

And then it was Ryker's turn.

Math in a Bow Tie

Ryker was the obligatory too-cool-for-school one. Math was a real drag, in his opinion. Once, as I was wandering around to see who needed help, I asked him what he thought of the current assignment. Not much, apparently! "You can dress it up in a bow tie, but it's still math," he replied. I smiled and walked on, thinking about my dad's ubiquitous bow tie and Ryker's charming metaphor.

On the last day of school he asked me a question. Never before had he done such a thing. (He was in my physics class too – that's where the question arose.) His need to have scientific notation explained outweighed his need to be cool. I told him how it worked, and for a split second, "Mr. Cool" was nowhere to be found. He was happy I knew, and I was happy I didn't blow my only chance to help him out.

Factor Rap

Mr. Hart (chapter 5) rushed in, saying he was there to watch the next one. He knew about it because it was filmed in his classroom. There was electricity in the air; he wasn't the only one who sensed we were in for a treat. Ryker and his teammates, Stella and Charlie, were on . . .

The movie begins with the teacher, played by Stella, explaining in a proper, teacherly manner how to factor quadratics. After a minute or so, she has to step out of the room. Ryker and Charlie play the students. While Teacher is away, they get bored and start rapping about factoring. They cover everything: the whys and wherefores from A to Z. Ryker is keeping the beat with a cowbell. Here's a sample:

Many a way to solve an equation
So I'll answer all the questions you're raisin'
Subtract whatever's past the equal sign
Once you find zero, you're doin' fine

Stella returns near the end of the song and discovers that all hell has broken loose in her classroom.

Teacher (angrily): What are you doing?
Students (guiltily): Well, we were just . . .

THE END

Shrieks of laughter from all of us. It was absolutely hilarious. The unlikely combination of math and rap music catapulted the performance into the stratosphere. This was more than great entertainment, however. A dreaded subject (for at least one of them) was in service of a passion, and the result was nothing short of sublime.

Turned out, Ryker's bow tie remark was no fluke. The guy had a way with words. What's more, a second truth was unveiled that day: he wasn't too cool for school.

After raving about the movie to the three of them, I asked the boys (they wrote the song), if they'd heard of Lin-Manuel Miranda. The looks on their faces – of sheer disbelief that I was wondering if they were familiar with the star composer-lyricist-playwright-actor-rapper responsible for the Broadway sensation *Hamilton* – was so funny. "Um, YEAH," they said.

Fifteen
Raggedy Pink Backpack

Angelica was late again. She wandered in looking like she'd just woken up and didn't have time to brush her long curly hair. She put her hall pass and iced coffee on her desk, and her raggedy pink backpack on the floor next to her platform sandals. "Can I go to the nurse?" she asked. "Yes, of course," Mrs. Simms replied (this was William the cartoonist's class: chapter 3).

When she returned, having been told she wasn't sick (and therefore had to stay at school), she and I got to work. Side by side, each with our own pencil and paper, we started the task of the day: graphing linear equations. Her favorite part of graphing lines was drawing, and then filling in, big triangular arrows at each end. She preferred to draw the lines by hand, rather than with a ruler.

She couldn't do much on her own, but she could simplify a fraction in no time flat. That was her specialty, and she was proud of it. Here's an example of how she did it:

$$\frac{12 \div 3}{15 \div 3} = \frac{4}{5}$$

And so she would find that $^{4}/_{5}$ is the reduced form of $^{12}/_{15}$. If she didn't already know what to divide by, she figured it out by trial and error. When the numbers were big, she did it in stages. Let's say the fraction was $^{75}/_{105}$. Numerator and denominator are both divisible by 15, but she might find $^{15}/_{21}$ first, after dividing by 5, and $^{5}/_{7}$ next, after dividing by 3. Curious about the skill that far exceeded her other skills (she wasn't "afraid" of fractions either, unlike most people), I asked, "When were you taught how to simplify fractions?" She knew *exactly* when: "In third grade!"

One Size Doesn't Fit All

Angelica was a senior, age 19, in danger of never graduating. Math was the main problem. Twice she failed the math section of the state exam, which students must pass in order to graduate. She was also failing math class – the slowest, kindest one there was. I began working with her at the side of the classroom; this went well, but didn't really resolve anything.

As a last resort, she was sent to the computer lab and set up with a hi-tech, fancy-dancy computerized math course.

Mary, Angelica's dedicated special education teacher, and I crossed paths one day. "How's she doing?" I asked. "Terrible! She's falling through the cracks!" Nobody was available to guide her. She was expected to do it by herself, and that was simply not going to happen because she refused to work and refused to put her phone down. I said I would ask if I could switch to the computer lab during that period; if not, I'd help her after school. Mary was incredibly grateful. I got the okay, and reported to the lab the next day . . .

The computer class was harder than her old math class! This didn't make sense: an inability to do even basic math on her own was the reason she was pulled from Mrs. Simms' class (the polar opposite of this one-size-fits-all baloney) in the first place. Approached conventionally, the course was useless for a student with Angelica's needs, but I figured I could adapt it. After all, the point, as I understood it, was to get through the math requirement come hell or high water.

A Knack for Multiple Choices

A couple of weeks later, Mary dropped by to check out our boisterous makeshift math adventures. She asked Angelica if she minded if she (Mary) told me what she (Angelica) said when she heard I'd be helping her get the math credit. (She had only recently learned that math was threatening to hold her back – a tearful discovery.) Angelica smiled and nodded, so Mary said she said, "I just love Ms. Bunker!"

Computerization notwithstanding, we still did the math the old-fashioned way: with pencils and paper. The look on her face when she saw HER ANSWER on the screen among the answer choices was priceless. I wish I had a picture.

Understanding how to rule out unlikely answers was part of it. I went over my crackerjack techniques, which run deeper than the typical advice to be on the lookout for answers that result from mistakes like multiplying instead of dividing, or putting the decimal point in the wrong place. She learned to recognize the traps that only savvy multiple-choice test-takers know how to avoid. All math tests that offer options to pick from tend to have the wrong answers written in similar ways. There's only so much the test-writer can do to an answer to make it look close enough to be tempting. Once you get the hang of spotting the illogical, the nonsensical, and the flat-out silly, you can usually skate past one or two of them – or sometimes, believe it or not, *all* the incorrect ones – before you even dig into the question.

She took to the trickery with lightning-bolt speed and gusto: "C is ridiculous! I'm crossing it out!" To top it off, she got to show me how to operate the program. As usual, my computer skills lagged far behind those of my student.

A listless girl was now a vibrant girl. Her hair was brushed. She wasn't late as often, and she hardly ever asked to go to the nurse. No doubt there were all sorts of unrelated reasons for these awe-inspiring changes (some of which, sadly, didn't last), but whatever the cause, she was looking radiant. I saw her bopping along one day, wearing her precarious platform sandals with some snazzy knee-high socks. She was chatting away, happy and carefree, on her pink cell phone.

I was giving her minor prompts and tips during assessments, but she was solving the problems herself. I was also playing the part of cheerleader, since without one, she would drift away and stop mid-test.

It was way too late for her to take math tests alone. Short of turning back the clock and beginning her education from scratch (with the personalized instruction she deserved!), the only compassionate thing left to do, I strongly believed, was offer her a padded shoulder to lean on as she hobbled across the finish line.

The powers that be, however, didn't quite see it that way: I got in trouble off and on for supposedly overdoing it. (Mary was on my side.) I was asked how it would "look" if she got A's after failing the previous class. "Maybe people will think she's finally getting the help she needs," I replied (earnestly, not sarcastically). Somewhere along the way, I offered to design a course for the struggling student, as an alternative. My idea was shot down immediately.

Finding ways for Angelica to succeed on the one hand, while placating authority on the other, was a balancing act. After one upsetting episode, I drove off in tears, changed my mind about a mile later, and drove back to school. No one noticed I was missing. Angelica wasn't in on the drama, but I'm sure she sensed that some of the life had been drained from our tutorials.

But still, she made it. She got the math credit, and she managed to pass the state math exam on the third attempt. What a relief. Other emotional and academic crises continued to plague her though. Her diploma was still in question *the day before* graduation because a few assignments weren't turned in yet. Finally, at the eleventh hour of her ill-planned education, it was decided that yes! she would graduate. I hope she was able to follow her dream of becoming a gym teacher.

FRACTIONS/*simplified*

By working with the girl who specialized in putting fractions in their simplest form, I was reminded to notice the simple, often fractional, moments in life. Joy can be found in such moments. It all happened in a nondescript computer lab, at a desk that was identical to the twenty or thirty other desks. Except that it was the only one with a pink cell phone in the far right corner (alerting its owner periodically with a tiny "ding"), a raggedy pink backpack stashed underneath, and a student who knew that answer choice C was ridiculous.

ACKNOWLEDGMENTS

Writers Cameron Morfit (my nephew) and Michelle Kuchuk (my daughter), and graphic designer Bob Brodeur (a friend), read early drafts and came up with suggestions that improved the book dramatically. I appreciate their time and expertise.

And many thanks to John Bunker (my brother) for the spectacular artwork: the Ticonderoga pencil on the front cover (tilted just so by the aforementioned Bob), the area-of-a-circle puzzle on the back cover, and "Shortcut to Pi" and "Pi Pie" in chapter 13.

AUTHOR AND ARTIST

Emily Bunker tutored math and the SAT for fifteen years; that was when she was Pencil Lady. She is currently a writer, editor, and book designer, and has a BA in anthropology from Stanford University. Her favorite pastimes include playing the piano (the only one allowed to listen is Jinx, her tolerant tuxedo cat), seeing plays (put on hold during the pandemic), and solving puzzles (any kind will do!). She lives on beautiful Cape Cod, Massachusetts.

Other books:

- *Horace and Elizabeth: Love and Death and Painless Dentistry* (winner of the 2021 David M. Little Prize for the best anesthesia history book of the year)
- *And She Felt No Pain: A Japanese Doctor, His Herbal Invention, and the First General Anesthesia in Recorded History* (in collaboration with Akitomo Matsuki, MD)
- *Crossroads Diary: Sushi, Tsunamis, and Elvis & other stories from Dr. Matsuki*

John Bunker, known as Maine's "apple whisperer," is a self-taught fruit explorer. He is also an artist and musician. Following graduation from Colby College with a bachelor's degree in English, he and some friends bought land in rural Maine, where they built log cabins and planted gardens. He's lived there ever since.

SONOMA SOURCES

Page 25 | Bones (accessed 12/17/18):

"Rhythm Bones," *World Beats* <http://www.world-beats.com/rhythmbones.html>

Rhythm Bones Central <http://rhythmbones.com/index.html>

Sue E. Barber, "The Bones: Ancient to Modern," *Rhythm Bones Central* <http://rhythmbones.com/sueBarberHistory.html>

"How to Play Bones with Dom Flemons," *You Tube* <https://www.youtube.com/watch?v=iMokBr9cTxM>

Page 26 | Closure (accessed 12/31/18 and 1/3/19):

Kevin Fixler, "Nearing closure of Sonoma Developmental Center, community envisions future of campus," *The Press Democrat* June 23, 2018 <https://www.pressdemocrat.com/news/8458300-181/nearing-closure-of-sonoma-developmental>

Lorna Sheridan, "Sonoma Developmental Center quietly closes its doors," *Sonoma Index-Tribune* December 31, 2018 <https://www.sonomanews.com/news/9122373-181/sonoma-developmental-center-quietly-closes>

www.ingramcontent.com/pod-product-compliance
Ingram Content Group UK Ltd.
Pitfield, Milton Keynes, MK11 3LW, UK
UKHW020420250726
13967UKWH00007B/2747